Fleeing Back

Pat Hanahoe-Dosch

FUTURECYCLE PRESS

Mineral Bluff, Georgia

Published by FutureCycle Press
Mineral Bluff, Georgia, USA

ISBN 978-1-938853-06-7

Contents

For Kathleen Dosch Flynn,
3/19/56–4/25/96,
and all the other ghosts who haunt these pages

Graves at the Edge of the Sea

From Galle to Colombo, the train
rails along the coast line of Sri Lanka
past cemeteries lining the strip before the beaches
at the edge where coconut palms and grass
give over to sand. The push and pull of tides. Or tsunami.
Graves the length of a few bodies away from the surf.
Remnants of Christians and Muslims.

Miles before Colombo, the city's fingers
scratch down the coastline,
homes of blankets stretched across rope,
strung between coconut or banana trees,
cardboard boxes. Scraps of metal. Plastic tarps.
King coconuts. Squatters
watch our passing on the rails.
We stare out the windows.
Faces. Plastic buckets. Palm fronds and sand.

Then the city rattles into focus.
A snapshot. A video. Intersections
of cars, asphalt, buses and trucks, bicycles,
motorcycles, three-wheeled open-air taxis.
Plaster and plastic Buddhas
sit at these crossroads.
Incense sticks. Votive candles.
An offering of a lotus lily.
A plaster Krishna, fading into gray,
stretches his arms toward a street's edges.
All of Colombo is grit. Curls of ash.
Pocked cement, steel, wooden shacks and
clapboard market stalls. Papayas. Bananas. Corn

and multiples of fish.
The civil war is over, but not
the hunger. Even the fat tourists,
who come for tea, gems, palm-lined beaches and the distant jungle,
are pulled to the edges of its tides.

In Sri Lanka,

if an elephant lumbers toward you,
step to the side of the road,
admire her thick, wrinkled legs,
skin crumpling in layers of gray folds,
the long, restless trunk with its
mottled pink, flared nostrils, the cracked,
leathery skin with occasional tufts of hair.

She probably won't notice you
as she makes her careful way
to the cooling river water,
a brief respite from dust, heat and insects.
There will likely be others with her.
Their attention will be on the road,
the water, and the men riding astride
their necks or walking beside them,
tapping their swaying buttocks
gently with sticks so they
don't stray off the prescribed path.

The Unnamed Ones

*For the 277 discovered buried in a mass grave near Brčko,
Bosnia, in 1992 and re-buried in another mass grave in 2007
with only 80 of them identified.*

leak into our tents
through the pores of the flapping roofs
and zippered doors, under
the tightly stretched
army cots as we lie still,
listening to trees scratching the air.

The unnamed ones
are in the vapors we breathe, in the burning trash,
in the green, foamy trench our waste water runs off
into the marsh, into the misty rain
before the deluge that muddifies
the ground around the wooden boardwalks
we navigate around camp.

The unnamed ones
are hungry ghosts, pulled
toward other stones engraved by families.
The river has digested all it can of them.
They leak through the mud and weeds
to reclaim their names in the voices of loons and owls,
but we hear only silence and birds.

The unnamed ones
are in the sparrows scattered by a few kicks
as they peck at crumbs under the DiFac tables,
the wasps we trap in plastic bottles
of sugar water, hanging from the limbs
of the DiFac tents,

the stray cats we trap and kill with poison to prevent unnamed diseases,
the mice glued to plastic trays and thrown away to starve.

The town below swallows its secrets.
We think we can make it vomit them up,
but only the river leaks putrescence,
only the river gives up its stories
but not the names. It will be 15 years
before we give them a place,
a marker for families' sorrow.
The river will have a new bridge.
New names will haunt the houses.

Metamorphosis: Letters From Asia

1.

The bus to Chiang Mai stops
at midnight
to let us stretch and eat
spicy chicken soup.
Dramamine clogs my blood.
Sluggish and
displaced,
I wander
between picnic tables
in this Thai version
of an all-night roadside cafe
toward latrines,
rows of porcelain
holes in the ground
with footrests to stand on,
a hose to clean with,
and I cannot use these
alien sinkholes.
I am *farang.**

We board the bus
again, thirty some
Europeans and one American.

The moon is a pair of hands,
cupped, begging alms.

We ride into Chiang Mai
with sunrise   fog rises

* The Thai word for foreigners, aliens.

over trees and rice paddies,
an army of spirits
rising from mud and green shoots
a barrier of mist
we drive through,
streets already thick
with cars, trucks and tuktuks,[*]
around the ancient wall,
through a gate and

descend
into morning air
stiff, tired,
guidebooks open to names
of guest houses and hotels.
I choose one
for the sound of its name,
Daret's.

That I have not thought
of you
for hours
has little to do
with you.

2.

In the ring
boxers kick and jump.
First blood goes to the fourteen-year-old.
I watch from one of twelve bars
surrounding the ring,

---

[*] A tuktuk is a public conveyance that resembles a cross between a motorcycle
and a rickshaw.

Mekong* and Coke, my companions.
The boxers lash out
with feet and gloved hands,
pummel each other
into the roped barriers
around the stage,
this not so different
from cock fights,
roosters flapping wings and stabbing
with feet and beaks,
the object, blood.

A man sits next to me, asks
if he can order me another
Mekong and Coke.
I say "sure"

but pay for it.
He does not know
how to take this.

The fourteen-year-old boxer
has won the match,
everyone claps,
there are splotches of blood
on his chest,
the other contestant's mouth
is clotted with it.
The winner
leaps over the ropes,
dances/kicks the air
around the ring,

* Both a river and a whiskey.

pumped.

This man beside me is Thai, speaks
English fluently,
wants only to touch
my breasts, his fingers already
stroking my thighs
beneath the table.
     I imagine what his tongue can do.
     He tells stories.
They are music
in his accent.

Tomorrow
I leave for the mountains, north.
He will stay behind.

3.

at 5 a.m.
   the monks come out
      in saffron robes, shaved heads
bare feet, they stand
   still, perfect-
      ly silent, holding
their alms bowls
   to offer
      the good fortune of giving
a karmic way
   of appeasing
      the laws of consequence

at 5 a.m.
the monks come out

i wander these streets
   in bare feet
      waiting for sunrise
drop a coin
   into an alms bowl
      the monk is startled
but cannot speak
   he must stand there
      rigid, silent, collecting
the day's
alms   the day's light
stains the sky   tosses
karma into the dust
of morning traffic

the monks are gone
by the time
i reach
my bed   i sleep
the temples hum with prayer
i sleep   i sleep

4.

riding the back
of an elephant is no different than—
no description fits
the bamboo chair is hard
to hold onto   the back of it
rubs and bounces into my back

the animal carefully
trudges along the steep mountain/river/jungle
path   surefooted and bored
i never thought

they had so much
hair, such rough & cracked skin
two hours of this

there are two of us
to an elephant
the man sitting next to me
is silent   in two hours
we have said nothing
my skin cracks under the silence
but what can we say
riding an elephant
toward the mountains of Myanmar
under a canopy of unknown foliage
and green   so many greens
of grass, of fern, of palm
of bile, of fecundity out of control
of plants I do not know
3 shades in one leaf
&

i reach out   pluck bamboo
tree branches and leaves
as we pass through
offer them to the spirits of this jungle
they brush my face and arms
as we move through
this lush swirl of feathery switches

the man next to me
ignores this   our thighs
stiff to avoid touching
in the sway and bump
of our passage

we cannot help touching
i try to imagine
the village we are traveling towards
but wood and vine
skin and knee   distract
the mountain grows beside us on both sides
we wind up a small ridge
my hands reach for a white blossom
red petals fall into my lap
the brush of a fern across my face
is softer than any human lover's

our thai guide sits perched
on the elephant's forehead
in perfect balance
occasionally tapping
the animal's neck with a thin
bamboo branch   calling ahead
to other guides who are talking and singing

the tonal words of thai
bounce along with the caravan
touch the river   rise smoke-like
in the mess of trees/bamboo/reeds/vines
and we follow   heading toward
a karen* tribe   whose people
are displays
in the museum of hill tribes
at the university of chiang mai

there are so many of us
farang   we are common

* A tribe of people living in the mountains of Thailand and Myanmar.

18

the villagers settle into their own
homes   we sit around
bottles of singha beer
on the floor of a thatched hut
woven walls   bamboo floors
the stars are hidden
by tree cover
& the haze of campfires
it is yesterday morning
where i used to be

tomorrow
we float down the mekong river
on bamboo rafts

5.
i am traveling with a man
we arrived here together
there is nothing between us
except an elephant   a jungle
a muddy river we swam in

naked
with natives   2 australians
4 new zealanders   2 swedes   2 italians
and an elephant
whose shit floated down the river
before us   we didn't mind

there are temple yards guarded by
stone demons   women
with bodies of birds
there are wats*   temples

* Thai temples, usually Buddhist.

gold roofs angled in flowing points
walls of glass inlay
air incensed with sounds of bells   sandalwood air   jasmine air
carved   painted   drifting
   buddhas   demons   spirits

a bamboo raft
and a river
between us

i float
the raft sinks
ankle deep
standing   straddling bamboo
as we flow on
i lose
my balance   fall
to my knees   soaked
i kneel and flow on
past opium farms
past jungle   past rice paddies
past other rafts   past old women waving
past stilted villages   past green opium bulbs of mountains
skimming the smoky blue not-horizon

the mekong flows in only one direction

to go on
       even to drown

is all i know now

Hong Kong, August, 1990

I rise into this sauna of morning.
Nearby, China squats like a pit bull
waiting for the perfect moment to rise
to its snarls. BMWs and Porsches crawl,
sparkling, between crops of high rises.

I ride the tram up Victoria Peak.
Buildings tilt backwards, but it is I,
rising along this mountain, who tilts precariously.
At the top, Anglo history displayed in sepia.

I go down, among shops and stalls
in this town of Western bargains.
Evening colors the sky like firecrackers.
Silk, lace, lamé and leather
in windows, bolts of it, or on manikins:
clothing, bags, shoes, discrete and indiscrete.
Tea shops, barrels of so many leaves
there is no distinct odor, and pots
of clay or silver blend among paper
canisters on papered, rainbow shelves.

Later, riding the elevator
to the 26th floor, to my hostel in the Chungking Mansion:
coughing smoke, dust and incense that rises
from restaurants and shops on the bottom floor,
fires, unsafe wiring, gas burners, grills, wood floors, frying oil.
Like so many before me,
I ignore what I'm gambling.

Outside, streets turn neon as night
takes over, crowds multiply

like ants around spilled fruit,
sifting in and out of open air markets and clubs.
I retire early from Oriental music,
clashing vowels and smells
of curry and trash that waft up 26 floors to my window.

I wince at the alien, guttural sounds of Chinese.
This is what *alien* means,
to be alone, 26 floors above a culture
eddying along streets between other
soot-blackened high-rises, a current
rising above commerce, politeness, silence.

Another Love-Gone-Wrong Narrative

Tonight's sunset over the East China Sea,
gold like Thai jewelry
and green as well as the usual
remnant pastels of a fading storm, clouds
the horizon with stretched wings
of incoming purples and violets.
I walk along the seawall to the bay,
follow the river it becomes, lapping its way
between hills lush with pines, ferns,
bamboo and vines. Night
settles like the black heron
circles the water, then,
wings spread, descends upon a branch, hops lightly
along the wood, folds his wings,
calls to his mate
foraging somewhere
out of sight. The shadows stretch the night
between, across a cluster
of Okinawan tombs
shaped like gourds or
expansive wombs, gates
to a parallel world
the locals guard against
with a handful of salt in a bowl by a door,
and statues of mythic lions
staked on a roof or
by a gate to frighten away
ghosts, spirits
of loss and grief and

I am not thinking of you.
That story.

Saving Face

1.

Gaijin. The word causes
the child's mother to frown,
to slap his hand as he points
to me, curious, certain
only that I am *gaijin, alien,*
eyes the color of the China Sea in a storm,
skin the color of dead coral.
He stares, ignoring
his mother who wants
to leave the store. He's not sure
if he wants to laugh
or keep staring. He smiles, instead,
knowing from his mother's response
he has done wrong
to embarrass everyone.
Face is at risk here.
I smile at him, say, *arigato,*
the least formal form
of thank you. The familiarity
more even than the implied insult
is sure to annoy, but
his mother smiles politely,
bows her head
slightly. The loss of face
is at risk,
even mine is important
in the face of her own.

2.

Billie and Stevie
if you read this,
forgive me,
I called you *Jews.*
At sixteen I didn't know
how beautiful the colors
of the sea can be
when they flow together
in the currents, how the changing light
between afternoon and evening
transforms the water, part blue,
part green, part gray, part silver
and all drifting, inseparable,
toward the depths
full of miracles and spectacles
I used to dream of
before waking into adulthood.
Now I have seen the China Sea
meld with the Pacific
above thriving coral reefs
where the water is a montage of sunsets.
Now my dreams
ache for those currents, the changing light.
I have been *gaijin.* Some days
I am always, still, *gaijin.*

And After, Then Again the Sunrise

This sunset is Thai gold on the China Sea,
water reflecting a delicate
24-karat softness. A gentle swell
glides over the reef, licks
concrete crosses scattered
like jacks before the sea wall,
extra barricades between typhoon waves and our homes.
This is typhoon season on Okinawa,
though now the sunset clouds
are the usual pastel greens, salmon, abalone, anemone.

Can you picture this?
I want you to hear the waves
glide across coral and lichen/moss-
covered rocks. Straight out
there's a wooden fishing boat,
flat-bottomed, narrow, with a solitary Okinawan
hunched in its middle, rod hanging over bow,
his net cast off the other side.
The smell of burning weeds floats across the exhausted air
from a nearby sugarcane field,
pungent enough to clear away snakes.

Across the bay, there are cliffs with caves occupied
by fragments of bone and trash,
painted with the scorching of fires.
One contains a marble slab inside
to commemorate survivors who hid there
during the typhoons of bombs, machine guns,
air raids of WWII. Before, it was a tomb: imagine
families huddled beside pottery bone jars,
each jar the size of a child,

bones and skulls tucked neatly inside.
Behind, a screen of bamboo and pine.
Beyond, coral reefs
stretched imperturbably before the tides.

The fisherman has pulled in his net, is rowing home.
The sky is all dark violet.
The sea is all gray, swelling to stronger rhythms now.
The swells will build through the night,
eventually engulfing
even the barricades
so carefully engineered to protect this beach.

Tell the Neighbors We Miss Them

New moon over Bali.
    It's yesterday in L.A.

Late afternoon. Rainy season.
    Banana leaves hang like umbrellas.
        The stars are veiled behind gray batik sarongs.

On Bali, nights are smeared with stars.
    Behind a palm tree, coconut rain.
        There's a monkey laugh.

A new moon means no dancing among the ruins.
    I have nothing to say.
        The stars are disappearing.

Spirits hide behind their hands
    like clouds. The Southern Cross
        has lost its right arm.

Allah chased the spirits out of Java.
    The Water Palace is dry,
        its ruins overrun with

chickens, dogs and batik shops.
    I said it's a tourist trap.
        The Southern Cross has disappeared.

In Bangkok, canals wind
    like sewers. In the wats,
        gold and stone temples, spirits hover

like incense smoke, fading,
    then scent of sandalwood becomes exhaust.
        When a monk in saffron robes

approaches for alms,
    will we salvage some
        good karma out of this pocket?

New moon in California tonight.
    We had a lovely time.

Saudi Arabia, 1995

I am driven by a man I barely understand
across the highway stretched through Riyadh
because here women are not allowed to drive.
On either side, dunes rise. Families gather
beneath the floodlight of a full moon.
The women, black moving objects
in their abayas and veils, cluster
like patches of night across the sands' white glow,
slipping through shifting ground.
Children run between food spread on eating rugs.
The night has draped its black silk
over the refineries that fence the horizon.

I am driven across the Saudi desert
by a moon that will not stop rising. If I howl,
would its white silk wrap like cords around my throat?
Would I choke on the voice let loose,
adrift across the desert's bitter skin?
One week until I leave
this country where I can be stoned for loving him.
I am grateful I do not.
Stone in moonlight is how I will remember him.

April in Versailles

Courtyards and gardens
whisper with shadows,
hordes of peasants at the gates.
History is a sharp guillotine.

What draws me here
is not just a voyeur's instinct,
not ghosts nor beauty,
nor even just art,
but an insatiable greed, a taste
for what it would be
to live like a queen.

Outside, on the roofs,
statues. A knight in armor
is almost poised, about to climb
through a window. I understand
his need. We'll crawl through glass
and blood even, with bludgeons,
raise sharpened shadows
to be on the other side
of those windows.
We'll eat cake till our blood
clots in sugar,
hungry for the residue
of such a delicate icing
we've never known.

Mt. Parnassus, Greece

Cicadas screech in the heat and cedars
so loudly the air scratches
as I breathe,
like grains of sand
ground between my teeth. Here

there are walls that once held
naked, perfect men
carved from rock, scratched and shaped
with the mountain's grit, much
older than Christ.
There are rocks older than the gods
whose shrines they encircle
like grave markers, like cairns.

Here a god was punished
for giving humans a gift
of fire. Today we burn
into ash and grit, screeching
like cicadas
shedding our skins.

Riding the Nile On a Felucca

The Aswan dam is its own colossus god.
In this modern period of Egypt
there are no more crocodiles,
temples have been drowned,
the sky has grown humid enough
to erode stones and monuments more completely
and faster than the sands of two thousand years could do.
But the Nile always flows.
Osiris, Nasser, Yahweh, Allah, Ramses, Jesus, Arafat, Bast, Mubarak.
The names and stories flow through the grass and papyrus
along the shore, the whispers of power and history like the hiss of a cobra.
Lotus blossoms drift. There are farms, mud villages, mosques,
children playing in the water,
and then just sand, rock and mountains, the burn in our sinuses
as we breathe the sun. The old kingdoms
sing to us from the valleys of the dead. The sands bind
their stories to the ones who walk through their shifting waves.
Ramses' head lies by his feet.
We are all fleeing plagues, running toward
the Red Sea, a pyramid, a tomb.
The Lotus Eaters
are the lucky ones, floating in oblivion.

Curse For a Man I Traveled With Who Left Me Alone in Cairo

May you forget Egypt, the blue nights
and the rhythmic sound of a felucca slapping softly across the Nile,
the temples to the gods lit like ceremonial fires across the shore.
May you never again imagine the shape of a goddess.
May you remember only the lips
of a camel drooling its refusal
to bend down and let you climb on its back
for the last of the journey up
Mount Sinai. And may you forget
the density of the stars,
the moistureless desert night
wrapped around you like a thick cotton veil
wrapped around a Moslem woman's head,
but remember only
the trash and broken rocks of the monument
to where Moses stood once upon a time,
and may you never, never remember
how it felt to feel the breeze like a god's
breath whispering
across your skin
when the first rays of dawn
stretched across the stone slabs, rock and sand of that desert's teeth
beneath the mountain.

Because the Timing Was Wrong

The air conditioner whispers
sounds like prayers. Though I know I won't
see you, I wait for your knock
anyway. We once climbed
to the top of Mt. Sinai
then back down to the desert.
At the peak, we held each other warm before the rising sun.
Between us lay our own stone tablets,
a wall of *Thou Shalt Not* bricks.

If there were a death ritual for the still living,
I would sit Shivah, or chant the Bardo Thodol,
to mark your passing, and then move on.
The air swallows wax
from a candle, the only light.
I breathe
dyed tallow. It is all I have left,
a souvenir from our trip
to Jerusalem. I picture
the Western Wall: unyielding,
unresponsive stone.

I will not pray. I will not
wail. I will not hope.
We are like the First Temple,
no longer even ruins,
only stories, rituals,
desires I don't quite know how to give up.

How We Become Mute

In my father's workroom, once,
    a forbidden place
        of wooden planks and nails,

you broke the door handle,
    locking us in.
        Don't tell, you said, *Don't tell*

as if my words could bring
    more trouble than you could bear.
        We fixed the lock ourselves.

Children. Husbands.
    We imagined ourselves
        a future everyone expected.

Now I like to think
    I'm free of all that.
        I've been to Bangkok and Bali, alone.

I kept your wedding present for myself.
    The wine glasses are broken now;
        I've replaced them with crystal.

Tell me, you say, *tell me*
    how you're doing. But continue
        how you never have time for anything.

Your oldest son is watching TV
    in another room. The baby
        is crying. You rock her.

I say, *Your children*
   are beautiful. The boys have grown
      so well, so tall.

So like their father, I think,
   as all three ignore us, caught up
      in Sesame Street's vowels.

We resort to tea.
   I bought it at Hong Kong's night market.
      Thank you, you say, *it's lovely.*

Fleeing Back

Floating down
the Mekong,
leaving behind
Chiang Mai, the petrol
smells and crafts hawked
in the streets, the starting point
of floating rafts and elephants
and trails that end
in temple bells, poppy fields and
rice paddies, I climb
tier after tier of green watery shafts
of plant shoots and mud
that capture the morning fog
in spirals and plumes,
waft moisture
toward awakening

into morning in New Jersey.
Somewhere a Buddha laughs.
I curl back into the mattress,
wrap myself around the spirals
of that dream, hoping to re-claim
the water around my knees,
floating back down the Mekong,
clinging to that raft.

New Jersey. Once I longed
for home, the Atlantic, the sand
of South Jersey beaches, the boardwalk
under my feet, pitch pines and the stark
acidity of the Barrens.

Now, I want desert sand, broken coral,
mud-brick ruins, palm trees and jungle green,
the Red Sea, the Aegean, or even
a river that runs through countries, dividing
opium fields and mountains.
How quickly I have grown tired here,
how familiar this life,
how comfortable, how impossible.

After Moving to Lancaster, PA

The sheep across the road are fenced in,
grazing across my neighbor's barbed barriers
with only an occasional, fleeting desire
for the higher grass growing at the edge
of the street, just beyond
reach; one caught his head
in the fence while trying.
The road must have smelled
greener, perhaps grass-sweeter,
and the gap just wide enough to gamble
on the size of his head.

Silos fragment the horizon behind
the apartment complex where I live;
barnyards, cows, green and brown
squares of patchwork
quilt the distance all around. Such stillness
settles here in the evenings when gray
dampens the sunset and dusk drifts like
dust raised in the draft of a passing truck,
creeping toward sheep, cows, you and me
and the mice burrowed in the field
an Amish neighbor has begun plowing
with horses strapped to a large machine,
trudging in straight lines, up and back,
tilling acres of straight furrows.

Evening draws lines
of shadows around me,
bindings I only dimly see.
I light a candle to chase away

mosquitoes, and shadows
flit for a while in the slight wind
across the mowed, yellowing grass.
Then lightning bugs take over,
like sparks scattering in the dark,
unable to catch flame.

Apology

To you the cold stones of Troy
were just another disappointment,
too rubbled of a landscape to cast on your imagination.
The beaches and rocks in the distance to me
were still pocked with shadows
of dead Greeks. In these stretched days,
now I've returned to the States,
I remember your face, perked like a cat's,
still hopeful, even as my train
pulled away with slight, hesitant jerks, then
finally, a surer rhythm. I left
again for another landscape
strewn with ruins too far gone
to reconstruct. How could I explain?

It wasn't the cathedrals of Barcelona or Seville
but the triumphant gestures of the Spaniards
who rebuilt my car's muffler from scrap metal
in a small village that smelled of olive oil and oranges,
nor the sight of Queen Hapshuset's temple
from my hotel window, across the Nile,
gold against the purple desert night,
but the call of the muezzins from the small,
plain mosque down the street at the moment
the sun first sparked the horizon and
the acrid taste of sand with each inhalation.

Even now, I grieve, though not for you:
how the gray cast of light across a wet branch
in February, in New Jersey, reminds me
of mud-puddled stones grooved by chariot wheels

lying beside broken statues, the smell
of coffee and cigarettes from a Roman café,
of Paris in rain, and stained glass windows
of a small church on the Rue St. Germaine.

What if there is no God?

That incessant pounding is the crash of water in waves
in Cape May, New Jersey, where sand and sunsets
are pale pastels, not the ochre flames,
the sand-burnt sky of Egypt or Iraq. Yet,
somewhere else, a muezzin cries a prayer, his pain
lost in the words. His voice rises like car exhaust,
the air fills with the refrain, a bargain—
There is no god but God—is that hope?
That God is sane and loving—despite any evidence—
Here, a priest says mass—
May you go in peace—
But it is all one pain, adrift
in sifting, wallowing sands,
for mercy and faith, on our knees,
the same prayer, the same hands
that stretch and grasp and sift
through the same fine particulates, abrasions and grit.

Of Elephant Turds and Poets

after Philip Dacey

The ten-year-old insisted
it was a blob of tar,
but her father knew
it was really an elephant turd.
Her mother thought of water buffalo.
This was, however, Pittsburg.

It was not, really,
that their existence was mundane,
but the father could only imagine
elephants in poems and zoos
and thought reality
could use a passing elephant
at least once in a life.

The mother wanted
Asia in dreams,
the hairy humped backs and spread horns
of water buffalo
moving through rice paddies
in a slow, steady trudge,
plowing deep through mud and green watery furrows...

The child was firm.
This was Pittsburgh,
the oval mass of piles
on the side of the road
was tar, and traffic
was picking up, rush-hour
zooming in. Time
to get off the road.

Betrayals

The sad plastic camels,
baby Jesus and Mary
are crooked, Joseph has fallen,
and the lawn is puddled with
grassless spots as if infected
with mange. Too much rain
this year. The small two-story cluster
of apartments is drowning
in gray sky. New Jersey in winter.
Far away, a giant wave
has consumed the coastlines of several continents
and more. Jesus is covered in mud.
My neighbor washes him off
before packing him away.
In the box, the plastic figures
huddle together so tightly,
when she pulls them out again next year,
her leavings from the divorce she just filed,
they will be cracked and dented from the pressure
and weight of so much
piled on top, box after box
wrapped in duct tape, shoved
far to the back of the closet,
the years' accumulations packed tightly,
stacked together, rising to a crest
as she sifts through the artifacts of betrayal.

Independence Day

It is the perfect Fourth
the July sun melts
the ice cream so fast there is no point
to putting it in a cone
scoops in cups and banana splits
are the favorites today
watermelons can't help
turning rancid and when we wish
on a firecracker its brilliance
drifts into sulfur and smoke
the humidity doesn't save us
from impossible clichés
like hot as the Iraqi desert
finally the last
Roman candle goes off
the last bus to New Jersey
is ready to leave
and we cross the river back
out the window
the red white and blue
lights of the Empire State
building light the horizon still
though eventually the bus takes us
past the Meadowlands onto the Parkway south

Last Night She Danced at the Blue Note

Today she walks off the subway
through a turnstile
up the stairs and out into
the filthy rain drenching
her skin and hair and staining
everything with yesterday's
dust and exhaust.
She is steeped
in clattering routine
feels the trains below
as she steps across the grates
along the sidewalk, faces
walk past and no one
hears the shriek of brakes
as a subway train stops,
lets off its passengers
in clots of more faces below.
She leans into the momentum
of walking through
the rain and through
the stoplight and on
toward the renovated
15-floor building, toward her office
computer and phone and e-mail and
one small potted Bird of Paradise plant
slightly brown at the edges by her desk.
Things die in this rain
she thinks, though no sirens
scratch the air right now.
She drips on the elevator floor

and ascends in fluorescent light.
Somewhere there is a shrill scream
of train brakes and the clatter
of people filing through turnstiles.

Oh Well

He says we are being exploited.
I say I would like, of course, to make
more money, but I like teaching.
He likes to lecture, and the subway steps
go down, but not all the way to the train.
The walls are cold and moist
and vibrate, like my body when things
reach a certain level, like the screeching
of train brakes in a subway tunnel when the
huge moving mass of metal and grime
grinds to a sudden stop
but the whole metal box
of people and glass shakes with resistance.
The smell is nauseating here
but yes, I agree, I say,
as we pass a woman wearing all of her
limited wardrobe with a bag of shoes next to her.
She is crouched in a corner; she adds to the
smell, and we keep walking.
I like teaching, I say,
but I'm thinking about his shoulders
and what if I could lay my head on one of them,
how strong would it be, how would he hold me,
but he is complaining about
egotistical intellectuals, and the subway train
is here, and then
I am waving goodbye.

And Now.

It begins
with fine cutting, the slivering
of skin from the thick layers,
the cushioning blobs
of fat, muscle and gristle
till, finally,
scrape of bone.

This is how Emperor Hadrian
condemned Rabbi Akiva
to death by flaying
him alive, separating
muscle and sinew
with a currycomb.

Whose hand will raise the first
gesture? The first brief
flick of fingers that signals
enough?

Did You Hear?

Some ADHD Hollywood agent
is now a New Yorker on my TV
in New Jersey, spinning publicity from DC
where he is receiving
some kind of award because, basically,
he is richer even than the stars he serves.
Leo, my birth sign, is spinning
toward the dark side of the planet now,
and a guy at Fuddruckers
who wants to pick me up says
Did you hear?
The liberals are all
liars out to turn us all
into socialists and fascists.
That's like being both Charlton Heston and Martin Sheen.
I tell him his TV is talking through his fillings.
He watches FOX, of course,
so I assure him
that I am part of the great liberal conspiracy
but, if he wishes, I would
be happy to bury him
in his Confederate flag or with
a bald eagle feather between his teeth.
Really, what I most want
is to give him
a dictionary.
You are the fascist, I say, *I am the socialist.*
It's like arguing with a 'shroom growing at the bottom
of a beer keg. The Hollywood agent
is beckoning with his middle finger

and static from the TV
seems to be spiraling outward
to claim the entire
room with all its bottles and glasses
scattered on shelves along the wall
as if we had just stepped on a UXO.*

* Unexploded ordnance.

Hydroelectric Irony

There is a waterfall inside the city
of Paterson, NJ, and it is
defiantly beautiful, like a falcon
hooded and caged in a room
of crumbling plaster walls
and office furniture. The rush of water
over rocks calls, the way
a raptor, released, throws its head
into the air, streaming its feathers,
traces dangling from its talons,
flowing molecules of oxygen,
feather and leather currents,

but the traffic as we wind around
the Passaic river
is all we hear anymore.
In an old photograph,
a rainbow appears across rocks
and turbulent waters,
but now the spindrift is gone,
the city is all
black and white, or sometimes sepia,
unless you look carefully
from route 80 toward
Garrett Mountain where
spring and summer foliage
hide the asphalt with borrowed green.

Paterson, 2003

From the vacant, nine-story rise
of bricked-up walls and bankrupt frames,
whole panes of glass fall
like knives from a drawer pulled too fast, slates
thick as guillotine blades, to slice through
the bones and shadows of passage below.

Church and Ellison streets are closed.
The wind has decided:
It's time to pronounce vagrancy,
half the block long
where the walls extend just short
of college classrooms, across the street
from the Board of Education,
blowing out panes
to shatter on stained and broken concrete.

This could be just metaphor,
the usual signs of inner city rot, but
someone lives
in the once-upon-a-time theater on the bottom
two floors. He removes
the board from a window
and crawls out, knees first,
at night when those streets
become already spent, hazardous objects.

Modern Koan

Your breath, the moment before you stop
at the end of hiking up Paterson falls,
the first look down from the bridge
to the cascades, that slight
lightness in your legs and the grip
of your hands on the ledge,
the froth and rocks
and water strong enough to stir
electricity from its chaos
even now, with the city dying around us,
and the car alarm you can still hear
even now, so far from the parking lot:
what does your friend, standing beside you,
hear beyond the drum of falling water?

Fantasies

In my dreams I love many men.
There, they love me back.

At first I am air, a tropical current,
shaping obstacles as I stream by,

cradling their resistance. We
fly into brightly plumed birds.

Together we are feather and bone in flight,
what we could never imagine ourselves. And then

I am driftwood emerging from a receding tide,
beautiful like beached bones,

ribs arched like an embrace,
my legs a scaffold over the dark, wet sea.

Stepping Off

But could you tell me, what is so terrible about stepping off the
end of a story?
                              —from "Afterward" by Anne Carson

In that ravine the slivered knives of refusal
carve out silence, *riposte*. For awhile. Then.
A Bridge of Sighs
to some *doge*'s cavern
of dirt, stone, and stench
of human detritus and betrayal.

Or. In the lengthening dark
a green canal
of thick, rancid water
snaking through a Venetian *campo*
diseased like a sewer.
Beyond, the *laguna,*
teasing with its promise of clean, open water.
An island of graves. A cemetery
where the dead look back
at another island
of churches lined with paintings
by obsessed Catholics in oils
mixed with powdered glass,
the frescoes, mosaics, sculptures
slowly sinking into fetid marshes.

But.
A boat pulls up to a *piazza.*
A light switches on in a villa beside the Grand Canal.
Later. A train pulls out of the station.

A woman heads back to Mestre.

The man in the seat beside her is heading for Trieste.

He offers her a *biscotti.*

Everything depends on her acceptance.

To a Male Poet Who Asked for the Secret to Understanding Women

A woman is
a poem you can never finish writing,
the rhymes never make sense,
the alliterations won't line up right,
and the metaphors always end up
as oxymorons. What would you give
for a secret formula,
the closed form tradition and male poets
have used to write their exquisite, tight
iambic panting, couplets and rondels,
madam sonnets, mistress villanelles?
Alas for you,
I am an elegy to what has been.
Reach close with your pen.
Open this new form gently.
What surprises beckon when
the poetic diction and images begin
to come, sweet juices
of accentual rhythms and long lines,
free, organic verse and internal rhyme,
the ending always tantalizingly close,
building, undulating with fine uncapitalized, unpunctuated
moments of exquisite, vibrant verbs and concrete nouns
you think you know
until you begin the next revision and a new draft grows
unsated, bewildering in its complexity and contradictions.

Marine Quoz

> Quoz: a noun, both singular and plural, referring to anything
> strange, incongruous, or peculiar; at its heart is the unknown,
> the mysterious. It rhymes with Oz.
> —William Least Heat-Moon,
> Roads to Quoz: An American Mosey

The kelp is crinkled along the tide line—the waves' castoffs.

The ocean foams at the edges, but the jetty rocks push back its passion.

In Margate, NJ, Lucy the Elephant's ass points downtown with her tail in
mid-shift.

Piles of tiny black mussels stink up the beach—the gulls are ecstatic.

The lifeguards can only see where the bodies drift above the surface.

The pure clear jellyfish are dead but still make our skin itch.

The word *conch* sounds like an insult even for a crustacean.

No one likes broken clamshells; the gulls scatter them extravagantly all
over the beach.

Quahogs are to mussels as field mice are to rodents.

Out of water, a starfish feels like a cluster of limp dicks in the hand.

The ice-cream man rings his bell from the bulkhead; seagulls circle above
him.

That wave is rolling with an empty Italian ice cup and a popsicle stick.

There is a sailboat out there somewhere; maybe the currents will bring it
close to our side of the horizon.

The lifeguards don't know they are watching us drown.

After Finding a Poem I Wrote for You Years Ago

In more than two decades since your death,
I don't think much of you anymore.
I have lived, Peter,
and well, or not well—
it all blurs now, the way
starlight and moon often did when I drove
too fast at night along a German autobahn,
too free of speed limits,
full of being foreign and strange
in an almost familiar place.

My chest, too, is a mass of wounds,
but I've healed; my body
is not empty and abandoned. I am
filled with more sins
than you ever grew to know,
and I have loved them all.
I have lived too close
to the zone of separation,
crossed back and forth between
Serb and Moslem territories,
living with NATO troops by a small town
of no remorse, mass graves, and other war crimes;
I have wandered the streets
of Bangkok, a woman alone
at three a.m., drunk, acting
only as witness. I swear
these have nothing to do with you.

I think I've finally settled
into my forties, in a job anyway,

and a place, committing myself
to hundreds of students whose lives
pass quickly through mine
but long enough
for me to turn with them
and point to another direction.
It's all I have to give, and never enough,
like the carnations we laid on your coffin,
like the poem I wrote then,
like this poem over twenty years later,
a handful of rice tossed on your grave.

Years Later

  For Kathy Dosch Flynn

Last night, again
I dreamed you were
standing on the bulkhead
between the beach and our street,
waiting, like fog clouding over
the island, waiting for wind and sun
and metamorphosis.

Some days I am sea glass,
sharp edges ground smooth
but no less brittle for such
wearing down. Today
I sit on the beach
and almost see you
by the lifeguard stand, walking
toward the water.
The violent buzz of a cigarette boat
drowns the sound of your voice.

I can almost hear you shouting at me.
I will not listen.
I would be sand
shifting beneath the waves,
erosion as movement,
not this shard of glass
ground down, shrinking before the tide.

I Want For You

(after Neruda)

the olive tree's gnarled reach,
swaying in a dry wind, rooted in coarse sand,
bearing and letting go its light fruit
for a heavy oil, twisting its arms
for a hundred years,
grasping the acrid taste of sky

nights of purpose, of fine sand
whispering under your careless feet
as you walk toward a welcoming shadow
under the moon, unwrapping its gray gauze,
and that you meet, the way moonlight sparks at the breaking
of the waves' last thrust toward the shoreline

earth's spinning gravity,
a way of placing each hand and foot
toward certainty, a sureness of rhythm
balancing you here, sure-footed and earnest,
anchored among a multitude of revolutions

and forgiveness,
the brine and quagmire of a salt marsh at low tide,
then the turn, the cleansing,
the rise of water, the flight
of herons and egrets,
a softening among the grass and reeds.

*Insh'allah**

In the space between 5 a.m. and awake,
from the Grand Mosque, the muezzin begins
the first call to prayer, the nasal tones
of his song that is not music
treble out, rising and falling
across the plaza, to meet
the tenored cadences of the muezzin
from the mosque several streets away,
and so on, accumulating, arabesquing
across the city in light cacophony
like the caress of your hands.
Waking, I remember
the calm purpose, though
the words, the details, are still
a language I can't quite grasp,
the meanings under
the dream's surface hinting
of the copper and gold
the morning smears across the horizon
like blasphemy, like forbidden fruit
smashed by tires, dripping rinds among asphalt and gravel.

---

* An Arabic expression that means "It's God's will" and is used to explain
everything from the philosophic to why you have no car insurance and when
the next bus will arrive.

Moments That Get Us Through

The pumpkin ginger scone with vanilla glaze,
with a slightly bitter aftertaste.

Rainfall of red-gold oak leaves,
the 7:00 a.m. light
touching the tips of the upper branches
as they sway the leaves off their skins onto the asphalt road.

The mild espresso smell of cappuccino,
its warmth under my bruised
hands, cold from gripping boxes
as I stored what's left of you away
in a cache closeted from sight today.

A five-year-old's rainbow,
colored laboriously within the lines,
but a glorious, cumulus orange sky
leaching its sunlight onto the purple grass below.

An unexpected hello from
no one I know as he
walks past in the Acme
where I anxiously hunt down
the last bit of bright orange
cheese doodles from the shelves.

Ode to My Heart

Greetings to you my heart,
receptacle of clotted oxygen,
wishes so thick with desire
they clot in my lungs and
fix a dark grip on
membranes, cells and capillaries.
I hack for breath.
This cough, O heart, is my
rib-cracking, esophagus-tearing love
for this copper-rich stain
of daylight I breathe,
staggering through each deep
arrow-ridden throttled movement,
but the nights, heart, the nights
I can almost just bear
you through the shadowed ether
into morning's lighter breath.
We are a pathetic couple,
doomed to a predictable ending.
Still, we bleed forward like a sunset over sand dunes,
a rust and copper smear into the yawning purple.

Stuck in a Hospital

I lie among
potted red geraniums,
purple orchids, fiddler ferns mixed with carnations,
all gifts to say,
"I'm sorry you're sick,"
meaning, "I am helpless to help you."

The plants stretch toward my throat with their stench.
Each breath from the plastic tube in my nose
sticks long pins into my chest.
I am a quilt someone is sewing,
squares of red and gold scraps
of someone else's life
pinned into my skin, waiting
the final stitching, a sharp-pointed gauze coverlet of leftovers.

No, my chest is such a pile of burning coals
someone could roast a pig over it,
barbeque-over-woman they would call it.
I'm the center of the feast.
Everyone asks, how did I learn to cook so fiercely,
with such passion and heat? This is how
Vicodin and an empty room
take the mind, slowly
(except, of course, for the flowery
stains in the air, their cloying scent
of colors leeching into oxygen,
settling like feathers around my face—or, rather,
like leaves and petals
falling onto pine needles: a crisp, thick mulch).

Heart of Lancaster Hospital

I am being released.
The doctor has signed the charts.
The insurance has guaranteed payment.
I peel off the ragged gown, threads unraveling
around the collar, thin immodest cone of frayed witness
to those sleepless nights filled
with lit corridors shining in the stale room,
the ringing of voices and phones
seeping like moisture, like air, through the curtain
surrounding the theater of my bed,
the dull Vicodin ache, the wasp sting
of the IV needles and blood tests and the relief
of oxygen, misting like fog
from the dual plastic stubs of tubing
that stopped the terrible coughing.

I walk, slow steps like
walking backwards on a moving sidewalk.
I grip my arm around the orange vase of red flowers
whose name I do not know.
I focus on one breath at a time.
My collapsed lung flutters
like a young bird wanting to jump from the nest.

I am released into the cool air.
It burns like smoke down my esophagus chimney.
I sit in my car and sleep.
To drive takes more fuel than my body can give.
I am an empty oil field, all wells depleted,
nothing left but sand and shards of metal and wood,
broken pieces of machinery released into brittle, corrosive dunes.

What sets wing under these blue-rimmed eyes,
under the spotted, bruised arms whose veins gave up blood so
    unwillingly?
What legs step finally into the bedroom?
What hands finally, finally, release the warm blanket from its watch post
at the edge of the bed and pull it up, gently, to rest?
What drug of starved exhaustion curls up and,
even now, after the blood clots that plugged my breath,
what in me denies, still, that I need you?

The In-Between Places

Wet dirt: roots and worms
tunnel a haven

such shelter in the dark
world of under there

where the songs begin:
the worms and seeds

compost in birds' tiny stomachs
from their feathered throats

hunger and desire blossom
into air and light: dawn

or false dawn and later evening
we rarely hear beyond

mating and possession.
A pigeon perches on my deck rail

for hours in a hard rain and wind
the water leaches through the down of his wings

his eyes are shut. He faces
directly into the deluge

In the gusting after-wind
he shivers away the remnants

and flies off to settle
in the thick branches of a nearby fir.

What Happens Sometimes in Starbucks

1.

He looked at me with coffee on his lips
and asked for cream, but what did I know
of innuendo? The Starbucks
seemed empty after he left,
but a teacher was grading papers at the table
across from me, and by the window
a slightly bald, fat man sat reading
The Wall Street Journal in a brown, stuffed and torn chair.
It is time, I thought, and picked up
my laptop, bought a coffee,
plain scuffed running shoes walking me carefully,
plain image of me in the glass door as I opened it,
plain, cold February burning my sinuses,
and a flat plain of black tar, the parking lot,
served up with rows of empty cars.

2.

Her blank look said, "What?"
So many coffees, so many
blank and empty tables, I have lost
count of the lost dates; the lost
spaces in the chairs unravel
tendrils across the café tables,
empty but for this cardboard cup.
It's not blank; it has a logo on it. I left too.
The logo is the image in the door
I walk through again.
My life seems logoed lately.
I haven't found the right slogan.

Just Because

your sister was mashed into
    bone and meat fragments
    smeared across a road and what was left
    of her car, you
cannot sleep at night until every
   neighbor's car is parked in a driveway or on your street,
    every voice next door is accounted for,
    every email has been answered, and
    every important letter and piece of business
is done and ready for everyone else to go on
if you meet a truck on the road
and it kills you.

Some of your neighbors lie awake at night listening
    for termites and carpenter ants and powder post beetles
    boring through wood and the impact
    of flesh against bone from the house down the street
    and the catlike howls screeching for police
because one neighbor long ago watched his father
    beat his mother to death and now he hears
    the clicking of coffin latches shutting out all
    finality of touch and he knows
    there are only termites and maggots left,
finally, to embrace us,
    and all he has left is a rage to stamp all the insects out.

The man who manages the liquor store five blocks away
and snaps your credit card through his machine
without ever cracking the plastic or the number
lies awake at night until his 16 year-old daughter
    sneaks quietly into her room, not realizing the last step at the top
    of the stairwell always creaks at the exact moment she thinks

she has made it safely back,
he dreams of a darkness so brittle
     it has already shattered and the molecules of glass
     shred his lungs so he can't breathe,
and he wakes rasping for air and the comfort
of knowing exactly where everyone he loves is, precisely,

but there is really only a dark house
for all of you, and the shallow relief of the alarm,
sunrise, a pot of coffee, and a car engine
warming up in someone's driveway the way it always has,
every morning you have lived here, no matter the weather,
or the day of the week, or even if that neighbor actually has a job
or anywhere else to drive to.

Conversation About a Third World Country

At the party
there were a number of bottles to choose from:
a dark red Sonoma Zin, a French Vouvray, a Napa Merlot,
a sweet Alsatian Muscat, an Australian Pinot.
Their host wanted a little variety in the wines.
The beer you had to bring yourself. There was cake
somewhere, and finger food, including corn-on-the-cob.
It was the Fourth of July.
I've traveled in third-world countries, too, a woman said,
in response to someone's story about his two weeks overseas
with a group building houses in a war-torn country.
I don't buy the idea we should pity them—they
are often happier than we are, she said.
Oh? Another woman said, examining a tray of thyme Gougères.
Yes, the first woman said, then stopped talking
to drink a mouthful of the almost blood-thick Merlot.
They don't need our form of civilization. It's patronizing
to shove it at them. She ate a slice of Brie.
They are free from the stress
of our materialistic, fast-paced lives. They usually
spend more time with family and have stronger
values, not wanting things
they don't know exist, like computers,
and so living happier lives, she said,
eating an almond. She smeared some dill hèvres cheese on a slice of
    flatbread.
But shorter lives, said one of the men in the group,
who passed around a bottle of Zin, re-filling glasses.
Poor or no health care, inadequate or no housing,
poor diet or even malnutrition, no indoor plumbing,

no electricity—you think those are easier lives? said another woman,
as she reached for a pig-in-a-blanket off the hors d'oeuvres plate.
The first woman finished eating a Swedish crispbread cracker.
If they've never had these things, they don't miss them,
she re-stated. At that point,
someone suggested they go outside to see the neighbor's fireworks.
They all wandered out to the garden
with re-filled glasses, just as the first Roman candle shot over their heads.

A Woman's Middle-Age Crisis

The electrician finished screwing
the exhaust fan to the bathroom ceiling.
They sure don't leave you much room with these wires, he said.
She wasn't sure what that meant.
I didn't see any signs of squirrel or mouse up there, he said.
There might be a hole under the roof though. They like to get in
and make their nests there. It's that time of the year.
Wonderful, she thought. She had been up most of the night listening
to scratching and rustling noises
coming from the closet with the hot water heater. She couldn't see past
the washing machine though. She put a couple of traps
and some poisoned bait
on the floor in there this morning,
but the sounds continued
until the electrician showed up.
Later, she stared at the holes
around the edges of the fan's screen.
He had cut a rectangle into the ceiling
though the fan was an oval.
The creature's clawing and scrabbling began again.
She lived alone. There was no one to call.
She sat on the bed with the lights on,
listening for the sound of a trap springing.

To the Westboro Baptist "Church"

1.

If America is going to die
sometime in this decade because of our sins, then
I raise a glass of Prosecco to our demise and toast
all these sins that brought us here, our idols of flag and Constitution,
what tolerance and equality, freedoms and rights we have
managed to build through picket lines and lawyers and prayer and
    apparently
irony. I mourn all the sins
I lacked time, inclination or opportunity to indulge in,
the street-corner highs, dingy bars, one-night stands and more.
I sip this sharp, fizzy wine in your name and mine.
Such crimes we are about to reap such drastic retribution for
surely must have been wondrous, full
of ecstasy, a rapture of its own kind
to inspire such a legacy of fire and thunder.
Will God smite love blind to gender or color,
ceremony and the blessings of ritual?

2.

I taste salt
as I lick this man's neck, his chest,
his fingers, his foreskin. Is it a sin
to love him? Then I will
gladly go in flames, breathe sulfur,
burn into ash from desire. I say
do your worst, demon of heaven,
of this strident picket line, of this rant and rancor.
Every moment I spend in this lot of sin,

this passion, this hymn
to life, is worth such Biblical breath of fire or ice.
Like this glass of Prosecco, we gather
so much wet light, such tiny streams of spirit
swallowed swiftly in sips
of sweet effervescence, the white grape, the slightly bitter aftertaste,
will linger on long after we are gone.

Acknowledgments

Grateful acknowledgment is made to the editors of the following publications in which these poems first appeared, sometimes in slightly different versions:

Abalone Moon, "Hydroelectric Irony"
Atticus Review, "A Woman's Middle-Age Crisis"
Confrontation, "Fleeing Back"
Marco Polo Arts Mag, "Marine Quoz," and "Ode to My Heart"
Nervous Breakdown, "Fantasies"
The Paterson Literary Review, "Betrayals," "Independence Day," and
    "Oh Well"
Paterson: The Poets' City. "Paterson, 2003" (An anthology edited by Maria
    Mazziotti Gillan)
The Poetry Super Highway, "And Now."
Quantum Poetry Magazine, "I Want For You"
Red River Review, "Of Elephant Turds and Poets"
San Pedro River Review, "Last Night She Danced at the Blue Note"
Switched-on Gutenberg, "Curse for a man I traveled with who left me alone
    in Cairo"
Voices, "Metamorphosis: Letters from Asia"
War, Literature & the Arts, "The Unnamed Ones"
The Wildwood Journal: "After finding a poem I wrote for you years ago,"
    "Because the Timing Was Wrong"
Without Halos, "How We Become Mute"

Special thanks to Madeleine Deininger and Seth Martin for all their advice and support.

Cover art, "Breaker on Bunker" by Stephen Candler (spcandler.zenfolio.com); photo of the author by Cynthia Sierk; cover and interior book design by Diane Kistner (dkistner@futurecycle.org); Gentium Book Basic text with Myndraine titling

About FutureCycle Press

FutureCycle Press is dedicated to publishing lasting English-language poetry and flash fiction books, chapbooks, and anthologies in both print-on-demand and ebook formats. Founded in 2007 by long-time independent editor/publishers and partners Diane Kistner and Robert S. King, the press incorporated as a nonprofit in 2012. A number of our editors are distinguished poets and authors in their own right, and we have been actively involved in the small press movement going back to the early seventies.

Our annual anthology, *FutureCycle*, combines poetry and flash fiction. The FutureCycle Poetry Book Prize and honorarium is awarded annually for the best full-length volume of poetry we publish in a calendar year. We are dedicated to giving all authors we publish the care their work deserves, making our catalog of titles the most distinguished it can be, and paying forward any earnings to fund more great books.

We've learned a few things about independent publishing over the years. We've also evolved a unique, resilient publishing model that allows us to focus mainly on vetting and preserving for posterity the most books of exceptional quality without becoming overwhelmed with bookkeeping and mailing, fundraising activities, or taxing editorial and production "bubbles." To find out more about what we are doing, come see us at www.futurecycle.org.

www.ingramcontent.com/pod-product-compliance
Lightning Source LLC
Chambersburg PA
CBHW070009100426
42741CB00012B/3169